ASTROLOGICAL TALISMANS

Create and Activate the Planetary & Zodiac Talismans

by

Jean-Louis de Biasi

Theurgia Publications
www.theurgia.us

Astrological Talismans, 2019, Copyright © 2019

Cover design and Interior Art: Jean-Louis de Biasi

All rights reserved « Theurgia Publications ».

No part of this book may be used or reproduced in any manner whatsoever, including Internet usage, without written permission from Theurgia Publications, except in the case of brief quotations embodied in critical articles and reviews.

Publishers: Jean-Louis de Biasi - Patricia Bourin

Theurgia Publications © 2019

2251 N. Rampart Blvd #133, Las Vegas, NV 89128, USA

secretary@theurgia.us

Made in the United States of America

ISBN: 978-1-926451-20-6

Discover our other publications: www.theurgia.us

and Amazon: goo.gl/RP4RdJ

CONTENTS

- Introduction _____ 5
- Time _____ 5
- Ritual Process _____ 7
- Symbolism of Colors _____ 9
- Selection of the deities _____ 12
- Deities _____ 19
- Orphic Hymns _____ 70

INTRODUCTION

The planetary and celestial talismans you will find in this book will allow you to connect your invisible bodies to these powers and positively influence your existence.

TIME

You can either choose to start with your natal chart, or by what is most needed immediately.

Natal Chart:
1st Option: You can choose to color and consecrate your talisman on your birthday. This is indeed the most powerful moment of the year. To do this, you will need to use the page of your birth sign, your ascendant and your dominant planet's page.
If you can, you should begin the ritual described below at the exact time of your birth. If this is not possible, if you do not know the time, start in the morning.
2nd option: You want to put this period of your life under good energy without waiting for your birthday. Choose to follow this process during an astrological sign corresponding to the same element as your birth sign. Consider the following table.
Fire: Aries, Leo, Sagittarius - Earth: Taurus, Virgo, Capricorn - Air: Gemini, Libra, Aquarius - Water: Cancer, Scorpio, Pisces.
Then choose a day of the week corresponding to your birthday. If you were born on a Thursday, choose an identical weekday. With regard to the time of day, apply what is indicated in the previous paragraph.

Specific action:
Use the list given below to choose the divinity that best suits your need and then proceed to the ritual.

Colors:
There are three possibilities. Choose the one you think is the most appropriate and feel free to experiment with each one. I remind you that this is the dominant color and that it is necessary to follow your intuition.
1- Choose the traditional color of the planetary deity.
2- Choose the color according to the desired effects. See Appendix.
3- choose the dominant color and the ancillary colors based on your intuition.
You can use the type of color you want: paint, colored pencils, inks, etc.

End Use:
Keep this talisman near your bed for the time it is used. When you no longer need its action, burn it. Do not store it. If it is a talisman linked to your horoscope, do not keep it for more than a year.

RITUAL PROCESS

After preparing everything you need to color your talisman, add 8 natural (or white) wax candles, a planetary consecration incense related to the planet or astrological sign, a white tablecloth, salt water and consecration oil (or pure olive oil).

Light your 8 candles.

Declaim:
>   Ô puissantes Divinités, je vous invoque avec humilité et amour !
>   Ô Êtres lumineux, que ce rituel soit accompli en parfaite harmonie.

Visualize your aura becoming more and more luminous.
Direct the palms of your hands towards the ground so that they are parallel to it. Look at the ground, become aware of the earth on which you stand and beyond that, of the entire planet. Keeping your hands in this same position, declaim the hymn of Gaia.
>   Ô GAIA, most honored Goddess. Mother of all blessed immortals, and of mortal beings, listen to my hymn.
>   I feel you at the center of all there is, I feel the pulse of your life when my feet tread the Earth.
>   Ô GAIA, you who nourishes all life, you cause everything living to grow, blossom, and fade; approaching in your luxurious attire, you spread your flowers sweetening the air with thousands of wondrous colors.
>   O young maiden of exalting beauty, you are the foundation of the cosmos. You are eternal. I worship you whose rich and vibrant breath carries perfumes rousing our senses. I pray you, come forth here at this very moment!
>   The sweet grass, the soft rain, flowers and everything that surrounds me sing your praises and manifest your presence.
>   Around turns the divine wheel of the stars; flux and reflux of all there is.
>   Ô GAIA, may you ensure that we receive your blessings in each season through the caresses of your body; may all the gifts that you possess be bestowed generously on each and every one of us.

Direct your thoughts to the Divine Powers and light your incense.
While the smoke of the incense rises, pronounce the invocation to all the gods:
>   Hear me, O Gods, you who hold the rudder of sacred wisdom. Lead us mortals back among the immortals as you light in our souls the flame of return. May the ineffable initiations of your hymns give us the power to escape the dark cave of our lives and purify ourselves.
>   Hearken, powerful liberators!

Dispel the surrounding obscurity and grant me the power to understand the holy books; replace the darkness with a pure and holy light. Thus, may I truly know the incorruptible God that I am.

May a wicked spirit never keep me, overwhelmed by ills, submerged in the waters of forgetfulness and far away from the Gods and Goddesses.

May my soul not be fettered in the jails of life where I am left to suffer a terrifying atonement in the icy cycles of generation. I do not want to wander anymore.

O you, sovereign Gods of radiant wisdom, hear me! Reveal to one who hastens on the Path of Return the holy ecstasies and the initiations held in the depth of your sacred words!

Place your talisman in the smoke of the incense for a few seconds.

Then dip your right index finger into the salt water and draw a cross with equal branches on each corner of the page.

Then invoke the divinity with the pronunciation of his hymn.

Now you should color your talisman.

When this is done, take the anointing oil and draw a cross with equal branches on each corner of the page.

Cross your arms, the left on the right. Breathe peacefully. Lower the head slightly and say:
> **May this talisman now be bound to me and bring me all the benefits given by ...** *pronounce the name of the divinity* **...!**

Be silent few second and then say:
> **So mote it be!**

SYMBOLISM OF COLORS

COLORS

As I explained in the introduction, the symbolic meaning of colors can be different according to which system you consider. If you want to use a specific one such as Qabalah, Hermeticism, or any other, find first the correspondences that are used. On my website, you will find Greek and Hebrew Qabalah correspondences along with the Hermetic system.

However, I want to give you below some elements about the connection between colors and personality. They can be linked to the Aura and to the spontaneous choice of your preferred color. They must not be considered as definitive or exhaustive. They are excerpts from my French book *Secrets of the Aura* that will be translated and upgraded in the next few years.

Red

Vermilion represents a benevolent power combining altruism and action. It is the manifestation of dynamic potential we can bring into our lives. This color manifests a mystical aspiration to the divine. It is an energy of strength, vigor and passion that can sometimes become hyperactivity.

Darker red characterizes an unbalanced dynamism. This energy could have been positive, but often leads to stubbornness and selfishness.

Very dark and brownish red manifest an intense sensuality, sometimes sly. It can be the mark of a latent violence, a strong egocentricity, or cupidity. Interestingly, red is also the color of anger.

Orange

When orange is shiny, it manifests a fundamentally positive trend. It is the mark of someone often thinking of others before himself. This color indicates a certain self-control. In a broad perspective, orange reveals a strong personality, character and intellectual development. This color also indicates a certain disposition to trade and easy contact with others. Orange shows tendencies to pride, loyalty, magnanimity, fortitude, generosity, nobility.

A very bright orange may indicate a tendency to tyrannical temperament and a waste of vitality.

Yellow

Golden Yellow indicates a high spirituality. This color is able to revitalize all levels of being.

Light and bright yellow are characteristic of someone who knows how to listen and talk to people. This color manifests tendencies to fellowship and happiness that comes from contact with others. This is the mark of an intense intellectual activity or ability, mental clarity and discrimination. This color helps to establish an emotional balance and clarity of thought.

Pale yellow may indicate a weakness of character, a shyness, or a need for privacy that will allow full and thorough communication. The degradation of this color can lead to a reddish yellow hue, indicating some weakness of mind and inconstancy on key issues.

Yellow-brown is associated with irritability. Yellow-red can also reveal an inferiority complex of which the subject can be unaware.

Green
Green is traditionally linked to healing and teaching.
Light green is beneficial. This color manifests a search for authenticity. Green has a feminine characteristic. It manifests a contact with spiritual plans. It is the mark of intuition. This color indicates a development of artistic ability and a use of creative imagination.
Green is the indication of a great deal of taste, a love of beauty and an understanding of the true and pure pleasures of life.
Green is also the mark of those who follow an inner journey that is not disconnected from reality.

Blue
There is a clear analogy between this color, the sky and the feeling of spiritual ascent. The lighter the hue, the more this spiritual aspiration is clear and obvious. It is the mark of beings who are progressing on the spiritual path. It indicates high and pure ideas. It is a sign of loyalty, sincerity and integrity. This color is linked to worshipping.
Blue is usually the indication of someone sensitive, emotional, and psychological. These individuals may love music, dance, and poetry. They are generally endowed with a very good memory.
When the color becomes darker, royal blue, and even navy blue, it intensifies the spiritual trends that we evoked earlier.
A very pale blue can be the mark of a weak person without great strength of character. However, this is the manifestation of a good memory and a general insensitivity.
Lavender blue may indicate an inclination for introspection and a will to work on the inner energies.

Purple
Purple manifests an active awareness of the spiritual quest already undertaken. It is the mark of an initiate into the mysteries. This color also manifests love and wisdom.
Shades of purple mixed with deep blue may indicate an interest for the occult world. It indicates good manners, charity, and respect for law and order.
For others, pale violet simply indicates an attraction for religions.

Indigo

As the previous color, indigo is the indication of high spirituality. It is more a religious attraction than an initiatic one. This color indicates a real search for inner truths that bring calm, serenity, and compassion. Moderation and balance are key words for this color.

Indigo also manifests a strong attraction to rituals religious and esoteric. When indigo is associated with a small amount of red, it indicates a practice of Theurgy. If this indigo is mixed with gold sparkles, then this spiritual is an essential part of the individual.

Black

It is difficult to say that black is a color. This is usually symbolically associated with evil and disease.

Gray

Gray is an indication of melancholy, sadness and despair. Gray is not as fundamentally bad as black. It is rather a manifestation of someone who indulges himself, and a lack of personal will. This color can be seen as an obstacle to real and constructive aspirations.

Pink

This is one of the fundamental colors of the emotional body. It marks refinement, solitude, fun, devotion, and friendship.

White

As you know, white is the sum of colors and mostly appears when the yellow and gold are intensely mixed. It is the mark of high spirituality.

SELECTION OF THE DEITIES

- Ability to express yourself in public (help you to develop your ability to express yourself in public) - **Hermes**
- Achieving (when we are experiencing difficulties in achieving inner peace) - **Pontos**
- Active (helps you to become more active) - **Athena**
- Acuteness (helps you to develop acuteness) - **Hermes**
- Adapt (increases your capacity to adapt) - **Demeter**
- Ambition (amplifies and manifests the characteristics of ambition) - **Helios**
- Ambition (helps you to develop your ambition) - **Athena**
- Analysis (helps you to develop precision and depth of analysis) - **Kronos**
- Anxiety (when we are prone to periods of anxiety) - **Pontos**
- Arts (to develop your love for the arts) - **Aphrodite**
- Attack (allows you to defend yourself from negative attacks) - **Ares**
- Authority (amplifies and manifests the characteristics of authority) - **Helios**
- Awaken (Whenever you are seeking to awaken the energetic forces of the universe) - **Ouranos**
- Balance (help you to find practical solutions to restore balance after conflicts) - **Athena**
- Balance (helps you in finding a balanced, centered path) - **Poseidon**
- Balance (helps you to balance your inner being) - **Hephaestus**
- Balance (helps you to find a good balance) - **Artemis**
- Balance (you may use the Arcanum to achieve balance in your life) - **Helios**
- Beauty (enables you to develop beauty) - **Aphrodite**
- Beauty (helps you develop a sense of beauty) - **Hephaestus**
- Being (to call upon a Higher part of your being) - **Ares**
- Beliefs (break you free from limiting beliefs) - **Ares**
- Benevolence (fosters benevolence) - **Poseidon**
- Benevolence (helps to develop benevolence) - **Zeus**
- Birth (allows you to give life) - **Aphrodite**
- Blockage (helps you to eliminate psychic blockages) – **Ares** (2nd aspect)
- Body (allows you to express your body more naturally) - **Aphrodite**
- Bondage (free you from bondage and chains that blind you) - **Ares**

- Bravery (allows you to develop bravery) - **Ares**
- Challenges (helps you prepare for challenges) - **Ouranos**
- Changes (helps you prepare for changes) - **Ouranos**
- Choice (allows you to sort what is best among all the ideas you have stored there) - **Apollo**
- Choice (helps you make balanced choices that promote harmony) - **Apollo**
- Climb (be able to climb the social and spiritual ladders with greater ease) - **Helios**
- Combativeness (helps you to develop your combativeness) - **Athena**
- Combinations (enables you to synthesize original combinations from several elements) - **Hermes**
- Common sense (helps you to develop your common sense) – **Hermes** (2nd aspect)
- Communication (helps you to find a better communication with others) - **Demeter**
- Complete (help you to complete old, unfinished projects) - **Gaia**
- Complete (can help you complete something you have been hoping to accomplish) - **Eros**
- Concentration (fosters concentration) - **Hestia**
- Concentration (helps you for problems concentrating) - **Athena**
- Concentration (helps you to find concentration) - **Hera**
- Conflicting thoughts (helps you when you are subject to multiple streams of conflicting thoughts) – **Zeus** (2nd aspect)
- Connect (helps you to be reconnected to the rest of the world and your environment) - **Demeter**
- Consciousness (To reach higher levels of consciousness) - **Aether**
- Control (gives you the capacity to gain control over what is happening at any given moment) - **Hermes**
- Courage (amplifies and manifests the characteristics of courage) - **Helios**
- Courage (find the source of courage and personal power) - **Helios**
- Courage (helps you to develop your courage) - **Athena**
- Courtesy (helps to develop courtesy) - **Zeus**
- Creative (helps you to be more creative) - **Selene**
- Creative energy (enhance your creative energy which is inside you) - **Ouranos**
- Creative imagination (to develop your creative imagination) - **Aphrodite**
- Creativity (helps you to develop your creativity) - **Hermes**
- Decisions (helps you for difficulties making rational decisions about a proposed project) - **Athena**

- Decisiveness (allows you to develop your decisiveness) – **Aphrodite** (2nd aspect)
- Defense (helps you to develop your defenses) - **Ares**
- Delusions (helps you to master episodes of manic delusions) - **Poseidon**
- Depressed (helps you when you feel depressed and down) – **Zeus** (2nd aspect)
- Desire (allows you to understand and assimilate the true nature of desire) - **Aphrodite**
- Desire (helps you to control your uncontrollable desires) – **Zeus** (2nd aspect)
- Desire (re-igniting the blazing force of desire) - **Eros**
- Desires (an awakening and expanding force that supports the realization of your desires) - **Eros**
- Desires (brings about fulfillment of desires) - **Helios**
- Dignity (amplifies and manifests the characteristics of dignity) - **Helios**
- Discerning (having difficulties in discerning the hidden elements of a problem or situation) - **Pontos**
- Dominion (amplifies and manifests the capacity to have dominion over others) - **Helios**
- Elegance (enables you to develop elegance) - **Aphrodite**
- Emotional tonicity (used to increase emotional tonicity) - **Zeus**
- Emotions (when we need to let go of certain emotions, entanglements, or situations we have been stuck in) - **Pontos**
- Energy (adds energy to your life) - **Athena**
- Energy (allows you to develop energy) - **Ares**
- Energy (helps you to control energy, and to generate it) – **Zeus** (2nd aspect)
- Energy (helps you to increase your energy) – **Zeus** (2nd aspect)
- Energy (re-igniting the blazing force of energy) - **Eros**
- Enhance (enhance your creative energy which is inside you) - **Ouranos**
- Entanglements (when we need to let go of certain emotions, entanglements, or situations we have been stuck in) - **Pontos**
- Exhausted (emotionally or physically spent) - **Helios**
- Fantasies (helps you to be rid of intrusive fantasies) - **Hestia**
- Fantasies (helps you to master uncontrollable fantasies) - **Poseidon**
- Fantasies (helps you to resolve fantasies that get out of control) - **Poseidon**
- Feminine (helps you to be in touch with your feminine side) - **Selene**
- Focus (helps you to be very focused in order to accomplish a single purpose or intention) - **Hermes**
- Forces (Reconnecting you with these natural forces) - **Ouranos**

- Forces (Whenever you are seeking to awaken, stir and use the energetic forces of the universe) - **Ouranos**
- Free (helps you to break free of whatever causes your difficulties) - **Ares**
- Friendliness (allows you to develop friendliness) - **Aphrodite**
- Friendship (helps create the best conditions for you to meet and make friends) - **Hera**
- Fulfillment (be able to achieve personal fulfillment) - **Helios**
- Generosity (allows you to develop generosity) - **Ares**
- Generosity (helps to develop generosity) - **Zeus**
- Generosity (to increase generosity) - **Helios**
- Gentleness (fosters gentleness) - **Poseidon**
- Goal (allows you to realize your goal) – **Helios**
- Goals (help you to change the circumstances that bar you from realizing your goals) - **Selene**
- Gods (helps you to receive the messages from the Gods) - **Hermes**
- Govern (the ability to direct and govern others well) - **Helios**
- Grounded (helps you to be more grounded, while dealing with the realities of the material world) - **Hestia**
- Guidance (helps you to find Divine Guidance in your life) - **Artemis**
- Habits (allows you to flow from one situation to the next, without staying stuck in ineffective habits) - **Hermes**
- Habits (assist you in eliminating old habits) - **Kronos**
- Habits (enable you to change bad habits) - **Selene**
- Harmony (help you find practical solutions to restore harmony after conflicts) - **Athena**
- Harmony (helps you to achieve harmony between yourself and the world) – **Hermes** (2nd aspect)
- Harmony Choice (helps you make balanced choices that promote harmony) - **Apollo**
- Heart's desire (figured out what your true heart's desire) - **Zeus**
- Hidden elements (having difficulties in discerning the hidden elements of a problem or situation) - **Pontos**
- Hidden powers (you need to increase your ability to manifest the hidden powers of your personality) - **Helios**
- Higher self (helps you to treat others fairly, with the inspiration of your Higher Self) - **Hephaestus**
- History (used to understand your past and personal history) - **Kronos**
- Honor (to increase honor) - **Helios**
- Honored positions (increase the aptitude for honored positions) - **Helios**
- Human nature (allows you to accept your true human nature) - **Aphrodite**

- Ideas (helps you to disseminate your ideas in a convincing manner) - **Demeter**
- Imagination (helps you to develop your imagination) – **Hermes** (2nd aspect)
- Impulses (helps you to free you from your impulses) - **Hestia**
- Impulses (helps you to control your uncontrollable impulses) – **Zeus** (2nd aspect)
- Incarnation (allows you to understand the meaning and purpose of your incarnation) - **Aphrodite**
- Initiatic path (helps you to find your initiatic path or esoteric school) - **Hera**
- Inner abilities (brings a state in which your inner abilities are revealed) - **Helios**
- Inner being (whenever you feel the need to re-establish contact with the inner and uppermost parts of your being) - **Eros**
- Inner peace (when we are experiencing difficulties in achieving inner peace) - **Pontos**
- Inner self (helps you to have a better understanding of the inner self) - **Hermes**
- Inner self (when we are trying to become most like your truest inner self) - **Pontos**
- Inner vision (helps you to develop your inner vision) - **Hermes**
- Insight (helps you to develop internal vision and insight in you) - **Hermes**
- Inspiration (helps you to find inspiration for some aspect of your life) - **Artemis**
- Inspiration (re-igniting the blazing force of inspiration) - **Eros**
- Inspiration (when we need to receive inspiration) - **Pontos**
- Intellectual mind (helps you to develop your intellectual minds) - **Hermes**
- Intelligence (helps you in developing acute intelligence and quick thinking) - **Apollo**
- Intuition (helps you develop a sense of intuition) - **Hephaestus**
- Intuition (helps you to develop your intuitive faculties during relaxation and sleep) – **Aphrodite** (2nd aspect)
- Invisible (allows you to conquer the invisible kingdoms) - **Ares**
- Isolation (helps you to correct a feeling of inner isolation) - **Demeter**
- Joy (helps you to increase inner joy) - **Artemis**
- Justice (helps to develop a strong sense of justice) – **Zeus**
- Justice (helps to develop justice) - **Zeus**
- Knowledge (helps you to assimilate knowledge) - **Selene**
- Language (helps you to develop the power of language) - **Ares**

- Life (helps you to learn the lessons of life) - **Selene**
- Listening (helps you to enhance your ability to listen to others) – **Aphrodite** (2nd aspect)
- Logical (increase the ability to use of logical analysis) - **Selene**
- Lonely (sustains you in your efforts, during periods when we feel abandoned and lonely) - **Artemis**
- Luxury (enables you to develop a love of the luxury in the positive sense) - **Aphrodite**
- Magick (helps you to increase the abilities for Magick) - **Selene**
- Meditation (helps you in meditation practices) - **Hera**
- Mediumship (when we need to develop and improve your skills of Mediumship) - **Pontos**
- Memory (helps you to develop your effective use of memory) - **Hermes**
- Memory (helps you to memorize) - **Selene**
- Memory (increases memory) - **Selene**
- Mind (allows you to do some tidying up in your mind) - **Apollo**
- Mind (To elevate your mind above the constraints and preoccupations of the material life) - **Aether**
- Music (to develop your love for music) - **Aphrodite**
- Natural forces (Reconnecting you with these natural forces) - **Ouranos**
- Needs (allows you to accept your natural bodily needs) - **Aphrodite**
- Network (enables you to create a network of relationships) - **Hermes**
- Occult powers (helps you to increase the abilities for occult powers) - **Selene**
- Old projects (help you to complete old, unfinished projects) - **Gaia**
- Optimism (allows you to develop optimism) - **Aphrodite**
- Optimism (allows you to develop optimism) - **Ares**
- Optimism (embodies optimism) - **Helios**
- Order (helps to develop the sense of order) - **Zeus**
- Organization ((helps to develop the sense of organization) - **Zeus**
- Originality (helps you to develop your originality) – **Hermes** (2nd aspect)
- Ostentation (to increase love of ostentation) - **Helios**
- Painful experience (enables you to release painful experiences in your life) – **Ares** (2nd aspect)
- Paranoid tendencies (helps you to correct paranoid tendencies) - **Hestia**
- Passion (allows you to express your passion) - **Aphrodite**
- Passions (helps you to free you from your passions) - **Hestia**
- Patience (fosters patience) - **Hestia**

- Pattern (allows you to get rid of outmoded personality patterns) – **Ares** (2nd aspect)
- Peace (enables you to find peace and a period of rest) - **Kronos**
- Peace (helps you to find inner peace) - **Hera**
- Perseverance (fosters perseverance) - **Hestia**
- Perspective (help you get a new or better perspective on a problem) - **Aether**
- Perspective (helps you to have a wider perspective on problems) - **Hestia**
- Pleasure (enables you to develop pleasure) - **Aphrodite**
- Poetry (to develop your love for poetry) - **Aphrodite**
- Pride (allows you to develop pride in good work) - **Ares**
- Pride (to increase pride) - **Helios**
- Problem (enables you to uncover the unconscious origins of present problems) - **Kronos**
- Problem (having difficulties in discerning the hidden elements of a problem or situation) - **Pontos**
- Project (helps you complete old projects, that have failed to produce fruit) – **Ares** (2nd aspect)
- Project (helps you for difficulties making rational decisions about a proposed project) - **Athena**
- Project (to develop planned projects) - **Aphrodite**
- Psychometry (when we need to develop and improve your skills of psychometry) – **Pontos**
- Purposefulness (helps you to develop purposefulness) - **Artemis**
- Rationality (increases the reasoning power of your rational mind) - **Demeter**
- Reality (used if we have a tendency to avoid reality) - **Zeus**
- Realization (embodies optimism and realization) - **Helios**
- Realization (increase the power to realize things, to progress to a goal) - **Selene**
- Reasoning (increase your power of reasoning and logic) - **Selene**
- Receptivity (helps you to achieve a form of receptivity that is open onto every dimension of reality) – **Aphrodite** (2nd aspect)
- Receptivity (opens you up to higher aspirations, by increasing your receptivity to the Divine) - **Artemis**
- Reconnecting (Reconnecting you with these natural forces) - **Ouranos**
- Refinement (helps you develop a sense of refinement) - **Hephaestus**
- Regenerated being (we can become a regenerated being) - **Helios**
- Regeneration (manifests the power of regeneration) - **Helios**
- Relationships (enables you to create a network of relationships) - **Hermes**

- Repress impatience (used to repress impatience) - **Zeus**
- Responsibility (helps you to develop responsibility) - **Kronos**
- Responsibility (to increase responsibility) - **Helios**
- Restless (helps you when you are feeling restless) – **Zeus** (2nd aspect)
- Result (to obtain an immediate result) - **Ares**
- Science (helps you to assimilate science) - **Selene**
- Science (helps you to develop your love of science and books) - **Hermes**
- Self (to reject that part of your nature that belongs to the "old self") - **Ares**
- Self control (helps you to develop better self control) – **Hermes** (2nd aspect)
- Self-confidence (allows you to develop self-confidence) - **Ares**
- Self-confidence (amplifies and manifests the characteristics of self-confidence) - **Helios**
- Self-control (helps you to develop self-control) - **Kronos**
- Selfishness (when we are prone to periods selfishness) - **Pontos**
- Sensitivity (allows you to express your sensitivity) - **Aphrodite**
- Serenity (when we are seeking serenity) - **Pontos**
- Seriousness (fosters seriousness) - **Hestia**
- Seriousness (helps you to develop seriousness) - **Artemis**
- Sincerity (fosters sincerity) - **Hera**
- Sincerity (helps to develop sincerity) - **Zeus**
- Sincerity (helps you to develop sincerity) - **Kronos**
- Situations (when we need to let go of certain emotions, entanglements, or situations we have been stuck in) - **Pontos**
- Skills (when we need to develop and improve your skills of Mediumship and psychometry) - **Pontos**
- Sociability (allows you to develop sociability) - **Aphrodite**
- Social (helps to best present yourself socially) - **Zeus**
- Social skills (helps you to develop your social skills) - **Hephaestus**
- Solutions (help you to find practical solutions to restore balance after conflicts) - **Athena**
- Spell (assists you to make spells) - **Poseidon**
- Spirituality (helps you to discover a personal expression for your spirituality) - **Poseidon**
- Splendor (to increase love of splendor) - **Helios**
- Stability (achieve stability on the material and spiritual levels) - **Gaia**
- Stabilizing (it offers a stabilizing influence) - **Zeus**
- Stir (Whenever you are seeking to stir the energetic forces of the universe) - **Ouranos**

- Strength (helps you when you need a quick boost in strength or energy) – **Zeus** (2nd aspect)
- Strength of will (to increase strength of will) - **Helios**
- Success (be able to attain success within the limitations of your abilities) - **Helios**
- Success (brings the manifestation of success) - **Helios**
- Sympathy (allows you to develop sympathy) - **Aphrodite**
- Synthesize (enables you to synthesize original combinations from several elements) - **Hermes**
- Tact (helps to develop tact) - **Zeus**
- Tension (when we are prone to periods of tension) - **Pontos**
- Think clearly (help you to develop the ability to think clearly) - **Hermes**
- Thinking (helps you in developing acute intelligence and quick thinking) - **Apollo**
- Thoughts (helps you to control your thoughts) – **Hermes** (2nd aspect)
- Time (enables you to have a real effect on the "time element" of your life) - **Kronos**
- Time (helps you to manage time and understand its influence) - **Kronos**
- Transforming (assists you in transforming suffering into joy) - **Hestia**
- Travel (helps you to travel with ease) - **Selene**
- Treasures (helps you to manifest the authentic personal treasures which we carry within you) - **Aphrodite**
- Trips (helps you prepare for trips) - **Ouranos**
- Truth (helps you to find truth) - **Hera**
- Unconscious (helps you to work on every aspect of your unconscious) - **Poseidon**
- Understand (allows you to better understand how other people function) - **Hermes**
- Understanding (helps you to have a deeper understanding of yourself) – **Hermes** (2nd aspect)
- Unfinished projects (help you to complete unfinished projects) - **Gaia**
- Upper reality (allows you to contact an upper reality located above the limitations of your reasoning mind) – **Aphrodite** (2nd aspect)
- Use (Whenever you are seeking to use the energetic forces of the universe) - **Ouranos**
- Useful (helps you to discover what is most useful to you) – **Hermes** (2nd aspect)
- Vital principle (enhance your vital principle which is inside you) - **Ouranos**
- Way of Return (when you want to make progress on the Way of Return) -

Helios
- Will power (allows you to develop your will power) – **Aphrodite** (2nd aspect)
- Will power (fosters will power) - **Hestia**
- Will power (helps you to increase your will power) – **Ares** (2nd aspect)
- Wisdom (increases wisdom) - **Selene**
- Word ((helps you to develop the power of the Word) - **Ares**
- Word (develop the Power of the spoken Word) - **Hermes**
- Words (helps you to find the right words) – **Hermes** (2nd aspect)
- Work (strengthens your capacity to work hard for long periods) – **Ares** (2nd aspect)
- Writing ability (helps you to develop your writing ability) - **Hermes**

ORPHIC HYMNS

GAIA

Ô GAIA, most honored Goddess. Mother of all blessed immortals, and of mortal beings, listen to my hymn.
I feel you at the center of all there is, I feel the pulse of your life when my feet tread the Earth.
Ô GAIA, you who nourishes all life, you cause everything living to grow, blossom, and fade; approaching in your luxurious attire, you spread your flowers sweetening the air with thousands of wondrous colors.
O young maiden of exalting beauty, you are the foundation of the cosmos. You are eternal. I worship you whose rich and vibrant breath carries perfumes rousing our senses. I pray you, come forth here at this very moment!
The sweet grass, the soft rain, flowers and everything that surrounds me sing your praises and manifest your presence.
Around turns the divine wheel of the stars; flux and reflux of all there is.
Ô GAIA, may you ensure that we receive your blessings in each season through the caresses of your body; may all the gifts that you possess be bestowed generously on each and every one of us.

PONTOS - OKEANOS

Hearken Okeanos! You the eternal Father, the imperishable, origin of immortals and mortals alike, you whose waves circle the limits of the Earth, hear my words!
Rivers, seas, and all of the world's gushing sources of water stem from you. Hear my hymn, o rich and joyous God!
You are the great purifier, you who limits the Earth and the cosmos, you who rushes forth in the waters, be propitious to me!
Always happy, come to the side of the initiate that I am, and watch over me with benevolence!

OURANOS

Ouranos, you who generated everything, indestructible element of the cosmos, hear my words!
Universal Father, o resting place of the blessed Gods, you are the eldest, the origin and the end of all; you turn as a sphere around the Earth!

You terrestrial and celestial guardian surrounding all, your motion is a roaring whirlwind.
In your breast is enclosed the ineluctable necessity of nature.
O blessed and illustrious Daïmon who sees all and engendered Kronos; you the untameable and variform God, you are of dark-blue vestments. Hear the voice of the initiate of your Mysteries and grant me a life of holiness.

EROS

O Eros, I invoke you!
You are great, pure, desirable, sweet, impetuous, skilled and cunning.
You are the powerful archer, winged, agile, running in the fire and playing with Gods and mortals.
The keys of the aether, of the heavens, of the sea, of the Earth, and of winds are yours.
The fruit bearing Goddess nourishing mortals and the master of the Tartar and of the raging seas recognize your kingship; you alone are the mover of the course of all things.
O blessed God, come to your initiate with a sacred voice and disperse away unworthy desires.

AETHER

O Aether, you are the home of the gods, omnipotent power of Zeus;
Blazing One, you govern the stars, the Sun, the Moon and give birth to everything!
O Aether, you who shines in the highest heaven, thou that ani-mates the cosmos, bright child, the stars shine on your body, showing your light to those who pray you.
I invoke you and ask you to keep me living and healthy.

HELIOS

Far-riding ruler of days, all-seeing arbiter of the planetary powers!
Thine is the wisdom of prophecy, the rapture of music and poesy, the upward surging force of mystical endeavor. Thine is the vision which sees beyond all change and chance, and the clear perception of truth which dispels all shadow.

In the rising and in the incomparable luster of the Day-Star thou givest a sacred image to magical ascendance, even as thy power enkindles a glory within us and elevates us to accomplish that which we seek.
Hail to thee!

SELENE

Hearken, O Divine Queen!
Powerful Selene, shine forth on this place!
You who circles the night and manifest your presence in the surrounding air, be among us!
You, maiden of the night, torch-bearer, magnificent star, waxing and waning, male and female, mother of time,
You, glittering silver light of the night, turn your gaze on ourselves and our works.
Splendid vestment of night, bestow upon us your grace and perfection.
May your celestial course guide you towards us, O wise maiden.
Come, you the joyest of all, and be propitious and in three ways shine your lights on this new initiate.

ARES

Hail to you, Ares! Indestructible and dauntless-hearted Daimon.
You the valorous, the robust, hear my words!
Weapons, wars, and the destruction of cities are all
manifestations of your power and passions.
O terrifying God, human blood and the clash of battles are your delights; the shock of swords and spears gladden your ears.
Most terrible God, you are also the one ending conflicts and discords, establishing peace and bestowing riches.
I praise you, take away from me any ills, and sweep aside any difficulties and conflicts appearing on my path.
O Ares, may the slanders, calumnies, and attacks I suffered and might still be a victim of be definitely brushed aside of my life. Send them back to those who acted malevolently so that balance be restored!
It is thus that Beauty and Divine intoxication will flow in my life, increasing the qualities and the strength I possess.

HERMES

Hear my voice, O Hermes, son of powerful Zeus.
You, the inspired prophet I listen to in the breathing wind,
You, swift herald moved by your winged sandals from Gods to mortals, be attentive to my voice as I sing your praises.
You are the one who solves conflicts, the one guiding those who reach the gates of death, but you are also the cunning God who loves profit.
You brandish the Caduceus, symbol of peace and power.
You, Lord of Korykos, who possesses the terrible and venerable power of language, come here and now before me.
Hear my words and grant me the gift of speech, of memory and, overall, a happy end at your side.

HESTIA

O sovereign Hestia, daughter of the powerful Kronos, hear my words!
You who reigns on the eternal fire lighting the hearth of our homes, consecrate your initiates to its mysteries! Keep them always young, rich, wise, and pure!
You who helps the joyous Gods and powerfully support mortals;
You the Eternal of a thousand forms, green and desirable, welcome my hymn and its offerings.
Grant me happiness and health, and may your soft hands bring this household under your auspices.

ZEUS

Hail to you, O Zeus, my Father. Hearken as I call you with confidence.
You are the one leading the courses of the stars with order and beauty.
You are the one shooting from the celestial arch the resounding and shining lightning.
Your resonant voice shakes the hall of the happy and your fire lights up the multitudes treading our world.
Tempests and storms go forth on your command as you brandish your luminous and swift thunderbolt striking the Earth.
Your fiery arrows terrorize the mortal failing to recognize your paternal power.

Fleeing your vivacious traits falling around him, his hair stands on end, frightened.
Wild creatures also hide and flee from your divine power.
Troubled, the divinities look up to your radiant face as the deepest folds of the aether reverberate your vibrant breath.
However, O Zeus my Father, your strength is the manifestation of life.
I recognize in your light, your voice, and your breath the manifestation of your power and of your love for your sons and daughters.
In this hour when your roar surrounds me, I offer you this libation.
Grant me your power, your shining beauty, your dazzling health, and your countless riches.
May your peace dwell in me and generate order and strength!

APHRODITE

Aphrodite, O smiling Goddess born of the sea, lover of the long celebrations of the night, source of generation, O you holy mother, hear my words!
You are the one from where everything proceeds; the one who gave us life.
The three kingdoms, the sky, the earth, and the sea, obey you.
As you sit at the sides of Bacchus, you preside to the feasts, thread the ties leading to marriage, and spread your mysterious grace in the lover's bed.
You are the secret Goddess slipping in the desire of men and women, silent she-wolf treading the night.
You are who all men desire, the image stemming from their soul, the magic philtre of their love and of the sacred ecstasies.
You who were born in Cyprus and put your foot on the pebbles of the shore, come close to me. Feel my desire to contemplate your perfect face, your perfect body.
You wander through the lands of Syria and sacred Egypt, and crosses the seas on your immaculate chariot pulled by swans.
O most happy and voluptuous Goddess, I invoke you and desire you. Ride the seas and come to me. Driven by the Nymphs' songs, come on the foam of the waves.
O desirable Goddess, may you manifest yourself to me at this instant. May I contemplate your naked beauty.
May these sacred words be pleasant to you as I hope my purest desire can reach the most inward folds of your being.
O Aphrodite, I invoke you!

CRONOS

Hearken, O Kronos son of the green Gaïa and of starry Ouranos, father of the gods, and of mortals!
You who orders the rhythm of time, you who are born, grows, and declines, hear my words!
You who foresees everything, hear my words!
You who resides in each and every elements of the universe, hear my words!
You who destroys and builds anew, you whose laws govern all, hear my words!
You, O Kronos, the ancestor of every living being, you the pure, the robust, the courageous, hear my words praising and invoking you!
Give heed to my call as well as to those who never forgot you, and bestow upon us, when the moment comes, a joyful and pure end.

ATHENA

O beloved Pallas, unique daughter that the great Zeus created from himself, Benevolent, powerful, and fearless Goddess, thou who help us in our struggles, hear my voice.
Thy kingdom stretches from the top of the highest mountains to the shady hills and peaceful valleys.
You who sometimes pushes the minds of men to commit follies, I recognize that you can be both terrible, strong and protective.
Thou you killed Medusa, you threaten the bad and protects the righteous.
Both female and male, you can create wars or reason.
You, born of Triton, who combated the giants with your father Zeus, you saved us from misfortunes and leads us to victory.
Hear my prayer, as I pray day and night.
Goddess with blue eyes, as I invoke you, grant me wealth, abun-dance, health and many years of happiness!

APHRODITE

Aphrodite, O smiling Goddess born of the sea, lover of the long celebrations of the night, source of generation, O you holy mother, hear my words!
You are the one from where everything proceeds; the one who gave us life.
The three kingdoms, the sky, the earth, and the sea, obey you.

As you sit at the sides of Bacchus, you preside to the feasts, thread the ties leading to marriage, and spread your mysterious grace in the lover's bed.

You are the secret Goddess slipping in the desire of men and women, silent she-wolf treading the night.

You are who all men desire, the image stemming from their soul, the magic philtre of their love and of the sacred ecstasies.

You who were born in Cyprus and put your foot on the pebbles of the shore, come close to me. Feel my desire to contemplate your perfect face, your perfect body.

You wander through the lands of Syria and sacred Egypt, and crosses the seas on your immaculate chariot pulled by swans.

O most happy and voluptuous Goddess, I invoke you and desire you. Ride the seas and come to me. Driven by the Nymphs' songs, come on the foam of the waves.

O desirable Goddess, may you manifest yourself to me at this instant. May I contemplate your naked beauty.

May these sacred words be pleasant to you as I hope my purest desire can reach the most inward folds of your being.

O Aphrodite, I invoke you!

APOLLO

Hearken, O joyous Apollo, you the Powerful, the Shining one.

Granter of riches, you who came from the black soils of Egypt, I invoke you as the priests of old by shouting 'IE'.

You, Titan carrying the bow and the golden lyre, Holy are you!

You who killed Python, light-bearer, Holy are you!

Shining and Glorious young man, you whose head is crowned by golden hair, Holy are you!

You who leads the Muses and the Choirs, Holy are you!

You who shoots arrows beyond infinity, Holy are you!

You, the oracle interrogated and prayed at Delphi and Didyma, Holy are you!

You, Lord of Delos, who sees everything and gives intelligence to us mortals, Holy are you!

Pure are your portents, and bright your answers!

You who contemplates from on high the Earth and its dwellers, listen with a benevolent heart my speech rising before you.

The beginning and end of all things belong to you, and there is no place, infinite or close, obscure or bright, which is not under your gaze.

The harmonious notes of your golden lyre balance the cosmos and the fates of mortals. Every sound and every ray of light is the manifestation of your divine harmony. Seasons succeed each other and the fields of Spring are gilded by flowers at the sound of your melodies.

O shining God of light and power, I am praising you as did the initiates of old.

Apollo, bright Lord, you whose voice touches me through the wind, you whose seal is set on the whole cosmos, appear before me at this instant as well as to every initiate singing your praises!

HERMES

Hear my voice, O Hermes, son of powerful Zeus.

You, the inspired prophet I listen to in the breathing wind,

You, swift herald moved by your winged sandals from Gods to mortals, be attentive to my voice as I sing your praises.

You are the one who solves conflicts, the one guiding those who reach the gates of death, but you are also the cunning God who loves profit.

You brandish the Caduceus, symbol of peace and power.

You, Lord of Korykos, who possesses the terrible and venerable power of language, come here and now before me.

Hear my words and grant me the gift of speech, of memory and, overall, a happy end at your side.

ZEUS

Hail to you, O Zeus, my Father. Hearken as I call you with confidence.

You are the one leading the courses of the stars with order and beauty.

You are the one shooting from the celestial arch the resounding and shining lightning.

Your resonant voice shakes the hall of the happy and your fire lights up the multitudes treading our world.

Tempests and storms go forth on your command as you brandish your luminous and swift thunderbolt striking the Earth.

Your fiery arrows terrorize the mortal failing to recognize your paternal power.

Fleeing your vivacious traits falling around him, his hair stands on end, frightened.

Wild creatures also hide and flee from your divine power.

Troubled, the divinities look up to your radiant face as the deepest folds of the aether reverberate your vibrant breath.

However, O Zeus my Father, your strength is the manifestation of life.

I recognize in your light, your voice, and your breath the manifestation of your power and of your love for your sons and daughters.
In this hour when your roar surrounds me, I offer you this libation.
Grant me your power, your shining beauty, your dazzling health, and your countless riches.
May your peace dwell in me and generate order and strength!

DEMETER

Deo, Goddess of a thousand names, you who are the mother of all things, Venerable Demeter, you who nourishes young men,
You who brings me happiness and riches,
You who grows corn ears and rejoices in peace as well as hard work, hear my words singing this hymn in your honor.
You who dwells in the holy valley of Eleusis, you who are in the corn when it is sowed, harvested, and threshed.
You live in green fruits as well as in every seed that can grow.
You are the one bringing to the living exquisite foods and riches; teaching them the gestures of nourishment.
You, the illustrious companion of Bromios, you the chtonian, friend of children and nurse of young men,
You, radiant torch-bearer, charmed by the sickles of Summer, hear my call and come at my side!
Harness your dragon-driven chariot and travel through the divine circles; joining me and shouting EVOE!
You who reveal your thousand forms in flowers and shining and sacred foliage, you the unique sovereign of mortals, appear now before me!
Fecundate my being, grant me peace, the order of law, riches and health!

HEPHAESTUS

Strong, mighty Hephaistos, bearing splendid light, unweary'd fire, with flaming torrents bright:
Strong-handed, deathless, and of art divine, pure element, a por-tion of the world is thine:
All-taming artist, all-diffusive pow'r, 'tis thine supreme, all sub-stance to devour:
Æther, Sun, Moon, and Stars, light pure and clear, for these thy lucid parts to men appear.

To thee, all dwellings, cities, tribes belong, diffus'd thro' mortal bodies bright and strong.
Hear, blessed power, to holy rites incline, and all propitious on the incense shine:
Suppress the rage of fires unweary'd frame, and still preserve our nature's vital flame.

ARES

Hail to you, Ares! Indestructible and dauntless-hearted Daimon.
You the valorous, the robust, hear my words!
Weapons, wars, and the destruction of cities are all
manifestations of your power and passions.
O terrifying God, human blood and the clash of battles are your delights; the shock of swords and spears gladden your ears.
Most terrible God, you are also the one ending conflicts and discords, establishing peace and bestowing riches.
I praise you, take away from me any ills, and sweep aside any difficulties and conflicts appearing on my path.
O Ares, may the slanders, calumnies, and attacks I suffered and might still be a victim of be definitely brushed aside of my life. Send them back to those who acted malevolently so that balance be restored!
It is thus that Beauty and Divine intoxication will flow in my life, increasing the qualities and the strength I possess.

ARTEMIS

Hearken, O Artemis, daughter of Zeus of the thousand names, roaring Titan of illustrious name, holy archer, you whose glittering torches illuminate us, O Dictynna!
Although not initiated to these mysteries, you protect those who give birth and appease the pains of childbirth.
O you who unties desires, friend of holy delirium, you who hunts with dogs and dissipates sorrows, hear my words.
You who hunt in the night, running swiftly, shooting arrows,
You whose subtle and virile form captivate my gaze,
You who welcomes, frees, and brings renown,
You, Orthia, Goddess of quick childbirth, nurse of young men, answer to my calling!

O venerable Immortal and terrestrial, killer of felines, you reign on mountainous forests! Holy and absolute queen, beautiful and imperishable flower, you dwell in deep and mysterious woods, you who likes dogs, Kydonian of changing forms!
Come, saving Goddess, loving, kind to every initiate, and give me the beautiful fruits of the Earth, desirable peace, and good health.
Hunt on the peaks of mountains every ills and sufferings!
O Artemis, holy huntress, be with me at this instant!

HESTIA

O sovereign Hestia, daughter of the powerful Kronos, hear my words!
You who reigns on the eternal fire lighting the hearth of our homes, consecrate your initiates to its mysteries! Keep them always young, rich, wise, and pure!
You who helps the joyous Gods and powerfully support mortals;
You the Eternal of a thousand forms, green and desirable, welcome my hymn and its offerings.
Grant me happiness and health, and may your soft hands bring this household under your auspices.

HERA

O Hera, from the purest aether to darksome hollows
Your aerial nature manifests itself to me.
Queen of all and blessed consort of Zeus,
You send soft breezes nourishing my soul.
Mother of rains, you nurture the winds and give birth to all!
Without you there is neither life nor growth!
Mixed as you are in the venerable air, moved by the whistling winds of the tides, you manifest your presence, and of all you are queen and mistress.
O blessed and many-named goddess, you whose kindness and joy shines on your lovely face, come at my side!
Bring me your goodness and your protection!

POSEIDON

Hear, Poseidon, ruler of the sea profound, whose liquid grasp begirts the solid ground;

Who, at the bottom of the stormy main, dark and deep-bosom'd, hold'st thy wat'ry reign;
Thy awful hand the brazen trident bears, and ocean's utmost bound, thy will reveres:
Thee I invoke, whose steeds the foam divide, from whose dark locks the briny waters glide;
Whose voice loud founding thro' the roaring deep, drives all its billows, in a raging heap;
When fiercely riding thro' the boiling sea, thy hoarse command the trembling waves obey.
Earth shaking, dark-hair'd God, the liquid plains (the third division) Fate to thee ordains,
'Tis thine, cærulian dæmon, to survey well pleas'd the monsters of the ocean play,
Confirm earth's basis, and with prosp'rous gales waft ships along, and swell the spacious sails;
Add gentle Peace, and fair-hair'd Health beside, and pour abundance in a blameless tide.